Stark County District Library
www.StarkLibrary.org
330.452.0665

OCT   2012

W9-ALM-710

DISCARDED

Unique Pets

POTBELLIED PIGS

Kristin Petrie
ABDO Publishing Company

visit us at
www.abdopublishing.com

Published by ABDO Publishing Company, PO Box 398166, Minneapolis, MN 55439.
Copyright © 2013 by Abdo Consulting Group, Inc. International copyrights reserved in all
countries. No part of this book may be reproduced in any form without written permission from the
publisher. The Checkerboard Library™ is a trademark and logo of ABDO Publishing Company.

Printed in the United States of America, North Mankato, Minnesota.
052012
092012

♺ PRINTED ON RECYCLED PAPER

Cover Photo: Getty Images
Interior Photos: Animals Animals pp. 5, 19; AP Images pp. 11, 12; Corbis p. 9;
    Getty Images pp. 7, 15, 21; iStockphoto p. 17

Series Coordinator: Megan M. Gunderson
Editors: Stephanie Hedlund, BreAnn Rumsch
Art Direction: Neil Klinepier

Library of Congress Cataloging-in-Publication Data

Petrie, Kristin, 1970-
  Potbellied pigs / Kristin Petrie.
      p. cm. -- (Unique pets)
  Includes index.
  ISBN 978-1-61783-442-4
  1. Potbellied pigs as pets--Juvenile literature. I. Title.
  SF393.P74P48 2013
  636.9633--dc23
                                    2012004889

Thinking about a Unique Pet?

*Some communities have laws that regulate the ownership of unique pets. Be sure
to check with your local authorities before buying one of these special animals.*

CONTENTS

POTBELLIED PIGS

What has four hooves and likes to hang out on your couch? It also loves mud and is very smart. Give up? It's a potbellied pig!

Pigs are mammals from the animal family Suidae. Their scientific name is *Sus scrofa*. Wild boars are members of this species, too. They are the ancestors of today's **domestic** pigs.

Pigs are friendly, smart, and cute! For these reasons, they can be fun household pets. What? That's right! Just like dogs or cats, pigs can be trained, walked, and cuddled. These intelligent animals can also open the refrigerator for a snack!

But we are not talking about a 600-pound (270-kg) farm hog! There are smaller **breeds** that make much better pets. One of these breeds is the potbellied pig.

A male pig is called a boar, and a female pig is called a sow.

WHERE THEY LIVE

Potbellied pigs have other names. They are also known as Vietnamese or Asian potbellied pigs. The **breed** came from the Mong Cai and I pig breeds found in Vietnam. There, the pigs lived in forests and woodlands.

In the wild, pigs are lazy! They love to **wallow** in mud for hours at a time. They also enjoy resting in simple shelters, such as dirt burrows.

Sometimes wild pigs put out a little more effort. They can create a **canopy** out of tall grasses. To do this, they clip the grass with their teeth. Then, they layer it with other debris. Finally, the clever pigs crawl under the layers to rest in their covered homes.

In the 1960s, farmers developed a dwarf pig from the wild Vietnamese **breeds**. Soon, this small pig was sold in countries such as Sweden and Canada. It

In Vietnam, wild pigs become active at night when the temperatures cool.

eventually became known as the potbellied pig.

Potbellied pigs were first brought to the United States by Keith Connell in 1985. These pigs were meant to be kept in zoos. But, people thought the cute little pigs would make great pets! Soon, potbellies were selling for thousands of dollars.

DEFENSE

In the wild, pigs have several natural predators. Larger animals, such as mountain lions and coyotes, hunt them. Pigs can defend themselves against other animals by using their sharp tusks or by running away. But humans present a different problem.

Humans are by far the wild pig's greatest threat. People clear land to build cities and create farmland. Factories pollute the ground, water, and air. These changes threaten the wild pig's way of life. People also hunt wild pigs for food and sport. In some areas, farmers consider wild pigs to be pests.

After the potbellied pig was developed, the Vietnamese government learned the **breed** needed protection. Farmers had started **crossbreeding** the potbellies. As a result, the **purebred** population had begin to decrease. So today, the government encourages Vietnamese farmers to raise purebred potbellies.

THE PET TRADE

Potbellied pigs are not wild animals, yet some have suffered unfair treatment due to the pet trade. During the 1980s, people were willing to pay a lot of money for a potbellied pig. So, pet retailers sold as many as they could. However, many new owners did not know or understand how to care for the pigs. So, many pets were abandoned or surrendered. Eventually, interest in pigs declined and demand decreased. This led to more responsible practices in the pet trade.

WHAT THEY LOOK LIKE

A potbellied pig is much smaller than the average farm pig. But, it can still be a hefty pet!

Male and female potbellied pigs grow to be 14 to 18 inches (36 to 46 cm) tall at the shoulders. They usually weigh anywhere from 70 to 100 pounds (32 to 45 kg). Although, many are known to grow to 250 pounds (113 kg)!

The potbellied pig has the same general body shape as most pigs. It has a round body and short, stubby legs with small hooves. Every potbellied pig should have a sagging belly and a swayed back.

A potbelly's snout is short and rounded. Its small eyes are blue or dark brown. Unlike other pig **breeds**, a potbelly should have upright ears

You won't know right away how big your pet will be. It can take up to five years for a potbellied pig to reach its full size. They can grow much larger than expected, too!

and a straight tail. If the tail is curled, the pig was **crossbred**.

Like all pigs, potbellies have thick skin covered by coarse, bristly hairs. **Purebred** potbellies are most commonly all black. Yet, they are also known to be black and white, all white, or spotted.

BEHAVIORS

Not all potbellied pigs act the same. Some are curious and playful. Others are stubborn and lazy! Some pigs show lots of affection. Others are

snobs! But one thing is certain. Pigs are very smart animals. This can make them enjoyable pets. They can learn tricks and can even be housebroken.

On the other hand, smart animals can get into a lot of trouble! A bored pig can destroy a lawn, furniture, and carpet by digging. What's all the digging about? It may simply be something to do. But oftentimes, pigs are using their snouts to seek their favorite thing. Food!

In the wild, pigs use their powerful, primary sense of smell to find food. They sniff and dig almost constantly. This is called rooting. It is a natural instinct for all pigs. This instinct stays with them as pets, indoors and out! If not allowed to root, your pet pig could become upset.

Pigs have poor eyesight. No worries!
They have a great sense of smell.

FOOD

Pigs are omnivores, so they eat both plants and animals. Roots, berries, and other fruits are favorites of wild pigs. They also eat worms and eggs. Some eat small animals, birds, and whatever else they can root out.

Domestic pigs will eat almost anything. Good choices for pets include soft vegetables such as lettuce. Breads and fruits can be included in their diet, too. Also feed your pig a low-fat dry food specially made for potbellies. This food should be high in **fiber** and low in **protein** and fat.

How much to feed a pet pig depends on many factors. Active pets need more food than couch potatoes. Adjust the amount of food to match your pig's activity level. A potbellied pig's belly should never be large enough to touch the ground!

Potbellied pigs can easily become overweight. Feed yours well, but resist its begging. Keep an eye out for skin rolls. These are a sign your pig has too much body fat.

The right amount of food and water is key to your pet's health. Your pig should be happy with two meals a day. Make sure your pet always has access to plenty of drinking water, too.

REPRODUCTION

Do you want piglets? Pigs can become parents when they are just five to seven months old. After mating, mother pigs are **pregnant** for about four months.

To prepare for birth, or farrowing, the mother pig prepares a nest. She wants a comfortable place to have one to twelve piglets! Four to eight babies is most common. Each weighs just 4 to 16 ounces (113 to 454 g). The tiny newborns must find their own way to their mother's udder for their first meal.

The piglets stay close to their mother for the first several weeks. Their mother's milk is their only **nutrition** during that time. After four to eight weeks, the piglets are **weaned** and switched to a diet of pig feed.

Once **weaned** and **socialized**, the piglets
are ready for adoption. They should be 10 to 14
weeks old. Before you adopt a potbellied pig, it
is important to find out if pigs are allowed where
you live! Some communities have laws that do not
allow people to keep pigs as pets. Instead, pigs are
considered livestock.

A mother pig's udder begins producing milk about 24 hours before her piglets are born.

CARE

Many people believe pigs are dirty animals. This couldn't be further from the truth! Pigs naturally go to the bathroom in the same place. Provide your potbelly with a **litter box**, and the pig will use it!

Pigs also have very little odor. You won't even have to give your pig a bath! Just brush it once a week to loosen dry skin. But what if your pig has taken a mud bath? Hose him down before letting him back in the house!

You will need to do some trimming for your pig. Pigs have 44 teeth, and 4 of them are long tusks. Trim these if they grow outside the mouth. Also trim your pet's hooves every 9 to 12 months. These efforts will keep your pig from scraping you or your things.

It is important to locate a veterinarian familiar with pig care. He or she can provide regular checkups as well as **vaccines** and medicines. The

Males that are not neutered are destructive, aggressive, and smelly! Females that are not spayed can be moody. They may also surprise you with lots of piglets!

veterinarian can also **spay** or **neuter** your pig.

Happy, healthy potbellies are entertaining companions. They can also be very challenging to keep. A bored or lonely pig can become **aggressive** or destructive. So make sure you pig-proof your home and give your potbelly the attention it needs.

THINGS THEY NEED

A potbellied pig's needs are basic but important. Your pig needs plenty of outdoor space for rooting. It also needs to stay cool, because pigs don't have sweat glands! So, they can become overheated very quickly.

Provide a shaded shelter or a pool of water or mud for **wallowing**. This helps keep the pig's body temperature down. Mud also acts as a pig's natural sunscreen, bug repellent, and skin moisturizer!

Pigs appreciate a good bed. Outdoors, they will create a cozy nest of leaves and straw. Indoors, pigs will use blankets to fashion a restful refuge.

Get a good harness for your pig. This will allow you to take your pet on walks with a leash. Sturdy

Consider adopting a pig through a shelter or pig rescue group. These organizations have many pigs in need of good homes.

food and water dishes will make mealtime less messy. And plenty of toys will help keep your pig entertained.

If well cared for, a potbellied pig can live 10 to 20 years. Some have even been known to live for 30 years! This is a long commitment. Their behavior can be more challenging than expected, too. So, be sure you know all about potbellied pigs before becoming a pig parent!

GLOSSARY

aggressive (uh-GREH-sihv) - displaying hostility.

breed - a group of animals sharing the same ancestors and appearance. A breeder is a person who raises animals. Raising animals is often called breeding them.

canopy - a protective covering such as the uppermost spreading, branchy layer of a forest.

crossbreed - to mate two different breeds of the same species.

domestic - tame, especially relating to animals.

fiber - a material found in edible plants that normally passes undigested through the body. It promotes the healthy functioning of the stomach and intestines.

litter box - a box filled with litter, which is similar to sand. Animals use litter boxes to bury their waste.

neuter (NOO-tuhr) - to remove a male animal's reproductive glands.

nutrition - that which promotes growth, provides energy, repairs body tissues, and maintains life.

pregnant - having one or more babies growing within the body.

protein - a substance which provides energy to the body and serves as a major class of foods for animals. Foods high in protein include cheese, eggs, fish, meat, and milk.

purebred - an animal whose parents are both from the same breed.

socialize - to adapt an animal to behaving properly around people or other animals in various settings.

spay - to remove a female animal's reproductive organs.

vaccine (vak-SEEN) - a shot given to prevent illness or disease.

wallow - to roll about in a lazy or relaxed way.

wean - to accustom an animal to eating food other than its mother's milk.

WEB SITES

To learn more about potbellied pigs, visit ABDO Publishing Company online. Web sites about potbellied pigs are featured on our Book Links page. These links are routinely monitored and updated to provide the most current information available.

www.abdopublishing.com

INDEX

3 1333 04092 7715